BERTHA COMES DOWN

Megan Pattie's writing explores subjects ranging from the Gothic, mythology, and the natural world, to food, mental health, and small moments of wonder. She is a previous Foyle Young Poet, and has been published in a variety of journals, as well as anthologies from Eibonvale Press, The Emma Press, Fragmented Voices, Dreich, and the Black Light Engine Room, who also published her pamphlet, *Tracts*. Megan lives with her husband in North Tyneside. They have a pet rabbit and two cats.

Also by Megan Pattie

Tracts (Black Light Engine Room, 2021)

PRAISE for *Bertha Comes Down*

Bertha Comes Down by Megan Pattie is an astonishing collection of poems which jolted their electricity through me as I read. The passionate, poignant and impactful collection comes at you with power and unflinching truth from the very outset. Lines like "...you do not turn around /in your madness and walk / out of it..." communicate a strength and self-knowledge of a poet looking back, in amongst and forward from issues with mental health.

The collection is filled with stop-you-in-your-tracks brilliance. It is a mouthfeel of well-planned rhyme and half rhyme, of rhythm and music, of consonance and assonance. It is gorgeous and rich in its language and lush with startling imagery speaking so eloquently of the body and the mind – tidal, urgent, and breathless one moment, shapeshifting into nature, then mythical and incantatory in another, then dark, measured and deeply thoughtful in the next. Moments of recognition often occur. Line like "As women will, /I dissolved into the walls" resonate greatly, and poetry is the means Pattie has chosen to write herself back into existence.

The poems move between weights – from air light to complex and dense, with Pattie artfully slipping in and out through the lines between. The poet looks both inwards and outwards – Pattie writes, "so shall you know yourself /unfurling boldly." This is a poet doing exactly that, bringing themselves to life through an amazing, enthralling, exquisitely painful yet positive, well-crafted series of poems which I thoroughly enjoyed reading.

—Jane Burn

In the shadows of these poems, Bertha, the presiding spirt, kindles fierce little fires that might galvanize a pale beast to life or burn down whatever house has wronged her. Bertha Comes Down is a book of transformations; a living grimoire with a gothic heart, bright as jet.

— Helen Ivory

Nobody writes like Megan Pattie. *Bertha Comes Down* is a deeply affecting and utterly shattering collection that came to me at the moment I needed it most. This poet blends an effortless mist of gothic with her signature flare for a stirring and savage emotional pulse. In a single word, this body of work is breathtaking, and everyone should read it.

— Lucy Rose

This is a bestiary, a spell book, a scream and a guide book to the underworld of the hurts that haunt us now. You will want to follow Bertha down into this beautifully crafted world and go 'hunting in the brine' - there you'll find a language, an utterance for all the wanting, breaking, losing and becoming that happens under the surface we call self.

— Carmen Marcus

CONTENTS

ISBN: 978-1-917617-63-5

Cover designed by Aaron Kent

Edited by Kit Ingram

Typeset by Aaron Kent

Broken Sleep Books Ltd
PO BOX 102
Llandysul
SA44 9BG

Bertha Comes Down

Megan Pattie

Broken Sleep Books

BERTHA COMES DOWN

Going mad is a process. It is not supposed to be the end result.
—Jeanette Winterson

A man is his castle, becomes it,
and I, the one who haunts.
So when I descended at last
from the attic, down the vertebra
of the halls, he felt it
in his own spine:
my imminence.

It startled him to see me
amongst the daylit rooms,
the furniture, intact.
He thought a woman
reached madness and stopped.

When I met the bewilderment
unspooling from his eyes
with, *I'm feeling better now*,
he thought I meant, *I'm back.*
His face, which had become
smooth circles of surprise, set again,
the pools of woolly confusion

were wrapped up and stashed,
and I saw him fold the months
away into an archive box, thinking
they would moulder to nothing
on the shelf marked *To Forget*
in some old cupboard in his head.

But you do not turn around
in your madness and walk
out of it, gathering up
all that has passed between
you and the unseen, eliminating it
with your good, sane hands.

No, you go on through it
as through a thick wood.
It will always be
a place you have been.
You will always smell the bark
and be picking bits of leaf
from your clothes, your skin
of fine bramble-scratch scars.

I think he understood, after a bit.
I could see it when he looked at me
and couldn't tell if my face was lit
with joy restored, as in a magic trick,
or if my eye-spark was a vision of fire;

I might go up again,
and the whole house with me.

TAKING

I'm folding my petals back into the bud.
I'm holding to myself, forming a fist.
My course up to now has done me no good,
so I'm through with giving; I'm keeping the rest.

I'm taking back my tears from the undeserving.
They can find some other balm to soothe themselves.
I'm taking back my heart—it needs preserving,
and I've made a space for it on the top shelf.

I'm taking back my hours from the wastelands
that turned my wealth of spirit to a dearth.
I'm taking back my treasures from dirty hands
of those who cannot even see their worth.

And why stop there? I'll take what was never mine.
I'll sweep up stars and starlings on the wing.
I'll take the sea and all that she enshrines.
I'll take the mountains, trees, each blessed thing.

I'll take all this and make of it a throne,
and sit atop my riches, out of reach.
All the world has, I will make my own.
I'll take it all and put it into me.

MOONCAT

Where she clicks at the throw of night,
making the soft dark luxuriant—
there the stars poke through.

She tumbles after the unravelling sea,
pulls back the tides in her silver claws,
only to release them with feline ease.

She stretches out the crescent of her spine,
curls into a shifting orb,
fur shimmering.

She has gathered sunlight in the jewel of her eye.
It glows through her sleeping.

SPELL FOR CONFIDENCE

Beneath a cloudy sky, turn over stones—
one hand, then the other.
Turn and turn, until the rain comes,
then grind the stones beneath the storm.

Drag your drizzle-damp fingers
through the dust; a murk of misgivings forms,
with which to smudge your doubts on paper
(best by a window
where gulls' cries rip the air),
then set alight before a mirror,
keeping your eyes on yourself
in the fireglow.

Save the ash and mix with soil,
iron-rich and staunch with clay,
in a pot of terracotta, and in this
plant a seed: the curlicue of calendula.

Await the sure shoot and burst of bloom,
remembering the blossom of flame

in your own eye. As the marigold
shows its petals without diffidence,
so shall you know yourself
unfurling boldly.

WEB

A silent wind-chime, a tatty chandelier,
a broken web dangling frosty leaves.

And the web shivered in raindrops
exploding in the wind's fingers.

And the web was full of flies,
in the eye of it like sunspots.

And the spider sat in the centre
of her work, and waited.

And the spider crafted it,
dreaming of the kill.

DARK TAXA

Radar blips
Pixel flicker gone out like candlelight

A tentacle thrums (somewhere)
in the deep and (somewhere) far off
at the edge of the web

a vibration a data rumour
old wives' tales out of the mouths of fish
mushroom omens
schtum

soil spectres

(some)   rocks skittering

down the mycorrhizal labyrinth

as the thread is yanked out of your hand

cryptic twitch

you will never   snap   your head around

fast enough to catch

we'll be found

when we want to be

found

THE KRAKEN

Futures unfurled
like tentacles—each more deadly
than the last. And there at the source I was:
a churning creature
of shrieks and teeth.

Knowing too well my own power,
I strove for stillness, sinking.
But in the washes of darkness,
the strikes of light,
the ocean stirred me.

I could not help but be shifted—
whatever ripples
I may begin.

OLIVES

They remember their primacy
in the firmness of their stones.

Ancient stories of hope, of peace,
rest roundly on my tongue
in softnesses of black and green,
and when I chew into the smooth,
sarcous resistance of olives,
I taste the salt of antiquity;
my lips are smeared
with sanctifying oil.

O to be holding
this power in my mouth.

The next person I kiss shall be a king.

MILK TEETH

A soft name for your starter set,
the cabal of hollow cowrie shells,
glinting in your mouth's pink pool.
One by one, they are making way,
these votaries, sometimes with blood.
You tongue serration, twist and spit.
There, they've fallen on their swords.
In your hand, jewels of augury
await the deeper, stronger force
that will push forth when the time is right,
and edge you with a saw of quartz,
and you will learn to bare and bite.

RUIN ON REIGHTON SANDS

It could have dropped from the cliffs above.

There was a staircase to the stone face,
a hash of pebbledash and bricks
strewn in the sand. Rusted struts.
Two wells, we thought, or gunposts,
where I left a stone that may have been
rose quartz in the very centre,
a seed of something that would grow
just from the latency of the place.

And where two walls had fallen
to mark a gateway, the strongest feeling
that should I step through
towards the sanderlings, toeing the tide,
I might not reappear on the other side.

THE DEAD FOX

Weeks later, the young fox
is still there, touched only by flies
and whatever in the air
assists the erosion of flesh and fur.

The council grass-cutters
have steered around it,
so a monument of neglect
rises—tall fronds and wild
leaves that wreathe and tend.

If you know it, then the heart
thrills with dread. The dead fox
is coming up ahead and you'll see
another week's progress
of decay and insects.

Your responses change:
the initial grimace and groan

to tired tuts, transforming at last
to a slantwise peer; eyes sliding
before you're in line
with the spot, its embroiling
haze of sharp aberration.

You wonder what new shape
the old death will take today.
You wonder when you'll see
the peeking secret of fox bones.

WILL TO BEAR

For an age monthly
I became entirely body.
No room for anything—
not even sight—but blood and pain.

I had to medicate my own nature,
and my biggest fear now is
all that ferocious will to bear
will be wasted by some cruelty of time
or biology, as if these two
do not conspire enough.

I hope to hold a life
in my life, then in my arms.
I will be able to say:

I have suffered for you
since your star was so distant

it could not be fathomed,

and I am strong enough now

to suffer anything again.

DAY OF THE CIHUATEOTL

In the late morning, I rise and wash
the blood from my thighs, the epitaph
of the death that brought me here.
At high noon, it is time to meet the men.
Embattled, our host of stolen mothers
take the sun into our ready hands
and walk it down to its bed of night.
Some of us sing lullabies, if we can bear it.
The day's work done, we stay up late
trading war-stories of cravings and labour pains,
inducting new sisters, their faces small
and livid within their warrior's regalia.
As the night goes on, I toy with
the hooked spectre of my left middle finger.
My face flickers skull-like in the fire.
I think of knotting snakes about my waist
and going down to the crossroads,
looking for children who have taken a wrong turn.

LEVERET

I am born into a grass cradle
perfectly the shape of my mother,
wriggling with kin, while over us
she flattens her ears down,
rests her chin on the matted earth,
so that she is the matted earth.
Through her, we hear the cry of the wind
and know the hawk soars on it.
I am born, full-furred,
with my eyes wide open.

THE SECRET

A secret is never old while it is kept.
You turn it over in your hands; it holds its shine.
The close air of the house through which you've crept
ripples with your twinned breaths of *This is mine.*
It is a vital thing and always fresh,
as air is living in the winds that run
and in the quick waves, water is refreshed
forever, while it is yours alone.

It wakes you in the night. You felt it there:
a finger-nudge, a haunting touch, a burn
which moves you to the window. As you stare,
the moon seems to regard you in return;
a whale's eye rolling on you in the deep,
while the secret shifts in you, talks in its sleep.

EVE IN OTHER GARDENS

Other eaves the envious wind will take
Other trees whose limbs I dread to touch
Other roots moss-coiled, disguising snakes
Other fruits that do not promise much.

Other Gods who may cast me out once more
Other gardens whose cankers I descry
Other sins I would not reach out for
Other Adams who will not meet my eye

SOLO TRAVELLING

Whitby, July 2019

Up cobbled streets, I do not know,
I wade through my anonymity,
brushing over me like voile or muslin,
teased by sea breezes.

All round the town and down
to the beach, I relish the fish-slip
of myself, breaching the scene
like a whale fin, glossy and rare
as a tailed star.

Here I am a stranger to everything;
something half-glimpsed,
they'll never be sure
they really saw.

CORMORANT

No lark, she is an old bird of the sea.
She sleeks her feathers down with water-slick
and soars her dark-drenched deep world shadow-quick.
As any sparrow up into the tree,
she dives down to the waves' obscurity.
She has no song, her voice is crude and thick,
and her body great and prehistoric.
Cormorant she was made, and thus she'll be.

Look when she holds her wings outstretched to dry:
an icon stands upon a rocky shrine,
resolute in her sea-soaked display
to leave the little birds their gentle sky.
She shuns their heights for hunting in the brine,
skims low over the water of the bay.

SPELL FOR WISDOM

Pierce lemon wedges with sun-warmed ears of wheat,
gripped in fingers slick with oil,
and with this quill of light, write
the alphabet of your innocence
on the petals of daffodils.

Wash your feet with the juice of plums
and wherever you walk, throw down
your nescient petals before you.

They bruise. Come evening,
the breeze will blow lavender,
whispering upon your lips
everything, everything
the wind has ever known.

OCELLI

At the lake edge,
the tiger drinking
flashes her ocelli.

Flick of ear and rise
her moon eyes.

Where her tongue touches
the water, her second sight

repeats, repeats, repeats…

MI O VUKU (A VUK NA VRATA)

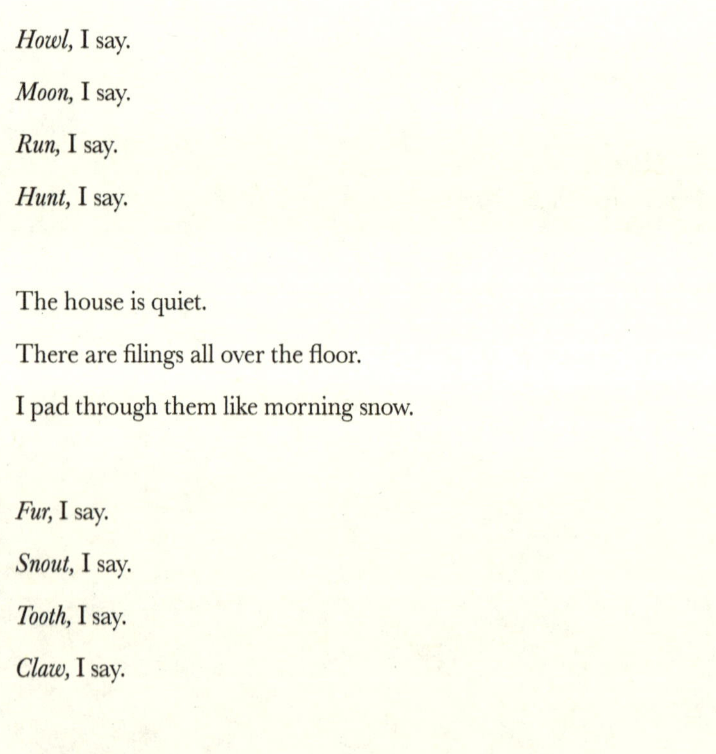

The house is quiet.

I admire my sharp nails.

I have been invoking wolves.

Howl, I say.

Moon, I say.

Run, I say.

Hunt, I say.

The house is quiet.

There are filings all over the floor.

I pad through them like morning snow.

Fur, I say.

Snout, I say.

Tooth, I say.

Claw, I say.

No more to stand by meekly.

I have so beautifully weaponised my hands.

SHE LIVES IN A HOUSE OF DOORS

A door that scrapes the floorboards.
A door with wide wooden eyes.
A door monstrously scored.
A door with a disguise.

A door with a glinting peep-hole.
A door with splinter teeth.
A door that remembers people.
A door you can pass notes beneath.

A door that rattles in its frame.
A door masked by a tapestry.
A door emblazoned with a name.
A door with an obstinate key.

A door abandoning its hinges.
A door that will not budge.
A door that shrinks and cringes.
A door with the look of a judge.

A door with a whining handle.
A door fret-and-filigreed.
A door that has known a vandal.
A door fixed fast with greed.

A door stopping its keyhole.
A door buckling with cracks.
A door admitting no hero.
A door hung with odd knick-knacks.

A door like a constant lover.
A door with a slow heartbeat.
A door half-hiding the sound of her.
Do not knock now. Retreat.

#MAGICMIRROR

My skin swiped smooth with pixel-dust,
with lips that suck the plump and blush
from all the lushest nectarines,
I slide light to the perfection of myself,
aggrandise my eyes to fairytales.
I declare it my dream, to be the reflection
of this refinement of my reflection.
I present my vision to a pale-cloaked sorcerer;
his collection of wands as bright and sharp as spindles.

ISOLATION TANK

Eleven

The water must be just right, so when you dive in
it is as though you leave behind your skin
and are boundless; your eyes opening
on absence, and your ears so wanting
they become inventors.
Suspended at the centre of beginning,
of this ultimate openness, I am,
moored in the possible, a peach pit.
I know not where I will end, nor what admit.

IN THE SILENT DARK

my pulsing aura thumps the air;
an aril of fear, rubbing
its fibres ahead into corners.

I can feel my listening
pulling out of me
like a spelk
out of skin.

He is always maybe in the next room
or at the bottom of the stairs,
and we move contrapuntally;
our fingers splayed in the dark
never meeting. A kind of crown shyness.

I wonder whom is driven madder by it:
me, the hunted aching to stop still,
or him, jaws twitching to slurp

the juicy terror from my goosebumps

and gulp me down, seed-firm and whole.

OLM

make a skill of stillness;
practise silence in the privacy
of pools. Olm keep themselves
rare as blazing pearls.

They will not come out of the water,
but have stayed submerged in darkness
for so long they grew eyeless.
They draw their own atlases;
an artless cartography
which maps the unfolding of years.

The few of us who saw believed
they had seen baby dragons.
Olm know better: they are proteus,
they are ilkless. They know
they are the anastomoses of time.

I imagine their hearts changed
to garnets in the spell of aeons,
as they outlasted ages
in the quiescence of caves
hewn of cold stone.

JELLYFISH

She wishes not to be a jellyfish:
a lightbulb always flicked on,
unstoppable brain
dribbling thoughts
in tangled strands.

Not to have this heavy head
she can only hold up
in the dark,
underwater.

Not to flounder on dry land:
ungainly blob,
tendrils trailing,
helpless.

Not to be
this plucked eye,
always weeping:

Do not touch me.

Please, do not

touch me.

CAVE

Leaves fall on fire and I am in your song
of tenderness and death, of love and gore.
Voices bait my soul, and all are yours;
daunting, soothing, each cries that I belong.

I'm your initiate, unknown to you.
I've come to learn my heart you are revealing.
I eat you up and find I have a feeling
of being swallowed myself: I'm eaten too.

Rapt, I crawl into you like your name.
Man, Creature, God, I come into your world
animal, a hungry, spellbound girl,
my neck bared for a kiss, a kill, a claim.

BREADMAKING

1.

I am golem, raw-form.
Thrown, knuckled, stretched,
wince-lined and howl-pocked,
until something awakens—
a resilience.

2.

Clean gingham tea-towel,
solemn as a veil.
I rest beneath:
my body mystic burgeoning,
with growth-aroma, the tang
of transformation.

3.

I have been through fire
and risen, firm as truth;
my insides all holed hagstone.
Should you knock, I am ready:
steam-sigh, crust-crack; I am
born to open.

THE OTHER COWS

Note our tender hooves and heavy heads;
meet our round, wretched eyes and you will see.
Flank on flank, we're all in the same bed,
transformed by divine lust or jealousy.

But what Io did, we never dreamed we could.
Clever girl, she got herself turned back.
Take a stick and score your name in mud?
None of us had ever thought of that.

That's how you can be restored again
should cowbell or a nosering keep you tame.
Take up a stick, your bloodied hands, a pen
and tell somebody that you have a name.

THE GIRLS

They came, given by a closing-down sex shop,
almost as grotesque in their completeness

as the man who was only a torso, for shirts.

They came made for lingerie and toys,
so the clothes looked worn by bones—

skin-tight jeans grimacing around the pelvis.

They came to us with weak knees and their broken
hairless legs are hard to hide—the calves

falling off at the barest touch.

She doesn't talk much, does she? men say
longingly, looking them up from feet permanently

tensed (oh to make them curl!) and down

from shiny hair, fake and full of tats around the pout
and paleness of the face. They ask if The Girls are for sale.

They don't know how I hold them to me to undress them,

to take them apart; how I cajole while dismembering
them—naked, bald, most desirable, most like life;

how I twist their two halves back together

afterwards, secure limbs, change hands.
They won't know the arms reposing in the store room.

I tell the men that The Girls are not for sale.

Over the shop floor, barren of patrons, The Girls
and I catch eyes. We hardly move, except

to adjust a wig or a wrist. We don't talk much.

GORGONS

There's a place in the town staffed by gorgons,
who drag their serpent-locks up into severe styles,
though the dry scales chafe.

Their hellos are drowned in hissing;
talon-nails tap at the till-keys,
and day long, beneath their gaze,
cringing customers scurry by,
desperately shunning
the mortification of meeting their eye.

In the throes of crawling hours,
each dreadful expression is carved
by stark store lights out of each face
as it passes, and the gorgons whisper,
This repulsion looks so like fear,
there must be a way to turn it into power.

When the whistle blows,

they flee beneath the shutters'

clattering fall, letting down their hair,

coming to hunt out your heroes.

THE OLD MASTER BY POST

An artist once sent me a painting by mail,
a subscription masterpiece that arrived in canvas scraps.

On the first day, I broke the seal
to reveal a slope of ermine skin;
on another, the moon of a heel.

He had his task; mine was to assemble
the postal puzzle that came one piece at a time,
so that to the very last I had to guess
what the hell it was the man intended.
In the shine of oils, I saw his knowing eye.
Sometimes I hated him.

I turned torment into moments of monstrous art,
and maliciously mismatched his model's parts
amongst topsy-turvy tongues of foliage;
a disfigured dryad whose eyes accused me
from the sting of florescence, the tips of sharp sticks.

I put the fragments back.

It was years before it was complete.
The shreds had drifted in with months between.

Finally, the woman lay, per his design,
in gorgeous dusk, amongst the cool of leaves.
And on the back, the tracks of tape,
the stains of wax, traced an art
that moved in murmurations
between his house and mine.

PART OF THE WOODWORK

After the photography of Francesca Woodman

No longer able to fight it,
I have become one with the house.
I was polishing one day,
and with a flick of the cloth,
there I wasn't. As women will,
I dissolved into the walls.

Now I grace the rooms: the curves
of my body in scalloped lace,
my laugh in the curtain cast
wide and splayed across the light.
I run through the floorboards:
acreak-aclunk, afuzz with dust.

I moan in the night.
I hold you as an armchair.

When I was a picture hook,
the plaster crackled, cracked,

my tack-eyes bursting from their sockets.
On the day I was the bathroom tap
I sang to be close to your hands.
I'm sorry about the flood.

Don't you remember my wet
silhouette on the floor?
Don't you feel my hot breath
in the clanking radiators?
This house is my work:
I am the windows looking back at you.

I am the mattress beneath
your blissful bodyweight.
I am your favourite teacup;
my perpetual pet lip
yearning until I wobble myself
clean off the table.

OLD TYPE

They make a home to come to
for the words that fled
from the tip of your tongue;
a haven for the obsolete,
a hell for slurs, afire with rust,
in dusty cases, or melted down.
Around the world, in the gaps
between floorboards, in the water,
all these aged alphabets, remembering their foundries,
hold silent court with all the words we've lost.

SPELL FOR VITALITY

In the morning, with the light
cutting through the kitchen,
on the shining counter
pour a glass of milk.

Sit with it for a while,
the glass of milk

with its little froth popping
until all that remains is cool marble—
a liquid pillar
casting its shadow across the surface.

Face the bright moon
of a blank sheet of paper
and tear it up, tiny tiny.

Grind salt. Grind chalk.
And blend all this to a pallid plaster

formed into two bowls.

In these place blades of grass,
snowdrops, fragrant needles of fir and pine.
Join the bowls and seal.
Now you have a quiet pearl,
hardening over its pith.

Wait for a clear, cold night
and seek out an aurora.
Beneath the dancing canopy of viridian,
cast your idle orb against the earth.

As air collides with air above,
stirring a monsoon that never falls,
the bare bead bursts,
spilling its vim and verdure,
and you will be awash with life,
feel it pushing through you—
the shoot that splits the stone.

COMMUNION

With

the curl of the conch

to my ear

I receive

a voice:

vascular ghost mollusc;

my selkie-self;

her swirling in the whorls of my body.

Through this sea-medium

(skin-coloured, like a lopped ear—

an earpiece)

we achieve communion

and she reminds me of the wildness,

the salt-bite in my blood

with a thump of her tail,

and whisker-zip

through to my fingertips;

reminds me

that as I listen

she is listening.

And though it seems she

arrives through static

waves rushing

worlds over,

when she tells me this story—

the flare of her voice

in the salt of the waves

in the wild of my blood

in the swing of her swim

in the rush of the sea

in my bedform veins

in the folds of my ear

in the curl of the conch–

The distance closes.

Almost I feel

saline breath

shifting the wet kelp

down on my cheek.

ACKNOWLEDGEMENTS

Thanks are due to the following publications and their editorial teams, where some of these poems have previously appeared: Butcher's Dog, The Blue Nib, Carmen et Error, *Co-Incidental 4* from The Black Light Engine Room Press, *Humanagerie* from Eibonvale Press, The Mechanic's Institute Review Online, Riggwelter, Snakeskin, and *Things That Go Bump in the Night* from Dreich Press.

Thank you to my mam, dad, and sister Cat, and to my husband David, who are so supportive of all my poetic endeavours, to Aaron and Kit at Broken Sleep for seeing *Bertha* and enabling me to make her the best she can be, to Gareth Ellis at Whitley Bay High School without whom no Megan Pattie book would exist, to Harry Gallager and P. A. Morbid for taking me under their wings and to the team at Inpress Books for being my cheerleaders!

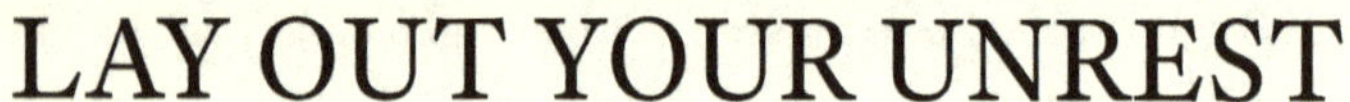

LAY OUT YOUR UNREST

www.ingramcontent.com/pod-product-compliance
Lightning Source LLC
LaVergne TN
LVHW051020080826
845145LV00009B/2714

9781917617635